Poems Of Judah Halevi

Charles F. Horne

Kessinger Publishing's Rare Reprints

Thousands of Scarce and Hard-to-Find Books
on These and other Subjects!

- Americana
- Ancient Mysteries
- Animals
- Anthropology
- Architecture
- Arts
- Astrology
- Bibliographies
- Biographies & Memoirs
- Body, Mind & Spirit
- Business & Investing
- Children & Young Adult
- Collectibles
- Comparative Religions
- Crafts & Hobbies
- Earth Sciences
- Education
- Ephemera
- Fiction
- Folklore
- Geography
- Health & Diet
- History
- Hobbies & Leisure
- Humor
- Illustrated Books
- Language & Culture
- Law
- Life Sciences

- Literature
- Medicine & Pharmacy
- Metaphysical
- Music
- Mystery & Crime
- Mythology
- Natural History
- Outdoor & Nature
- Philosophy
- Poetry
- Political Science
- Science
- Psychiatry & Psychology
- Reference
- Religion & Spiritualism
- Rhetoric
- Sacred Books
- Science Fiction
- Science & Technology
- Self-Help
- Social Sciences
- Symbolism
- Theatre & Drama
- Theology
- Travel & Explorations
- War & Military
- Women
- Yoga
- *Plus Much More!*

We kindly invite you to view our catalog list at:
http://www.kessinger.net

POEMS OF JUDAH HALEVI

ODE TO ZION

Art thou not, Zion, fain
To send forth greetings from thy sacred rock
Unto thy captive train,
Who greet thee as the remnants of thy flock?
Take thou on every side —
East, west, and south, and north — their greetings multi-
    plied.
Sadly he greets thee still,
The prisoner of hope, who, day and night,
Sheds ceaseless tears, like dew on Hermon's hill —
Would that they fell upon thy mountain's height!

Harsh is my voice when I bewail thy woes,
But when in fancy's dream
I see thy freedom, forth its cadence flows
Sweet as the harps that hung by Babel's stream.
My heart is sore distressed
For Bethel ever blessed,
For Peniel, and each ancient, sacred place.
The holy presence there
To thee is present where
Thy Maker opes thy gates, the gates of heaven to face.

The glory of the Lord will ever be
Thy sole and perfect light;
No need hast thou, then, to illumine thee,
Of sun by day, or moon and stars by night.
I would that, where God's spirit was of yore
Poured out unto thy holy ones, I might
There, too, my soul outpour!
The house of kings and throne of God wert thou,

How comes of it then that now
Slaves fill the throne where sat thy kings before?

Oh! who will lead me on
To seek the posts where, in far-distant years,
The angels in their glory dawned upon
Thy messengers and seers?
Oh! who will give me wings
That I may fly away,
And there, at rest from all my wanderings,
The ruins of my heart among thy ruins lay?
I'll bend my face unto thy soil, and hold
Thy stones as precious gold.
And when in Hebron I have stood beside
My fathers' tombs, then will I pass in turn
Thy plains and forest wide,
Until I stand on Gilead and discern
Mount Hor and Mount Abarim, 'neath whose crest
Thy luminaries twain, thy guides and beacons rest.

Thy air is life unto my soul, thy grains
Of dust are myrrh, thy streams with honey flow;
Naked and barefoot, to thy ruined fanes
How gladly would I go;
To where the ark was treasured, and in dim
Recesses dwelt the holy cherubim.

I rend the beauty of my locks, and cry
In bitter wrath against the cruel fate
That bids thy holy Nazarites to lie
In earth contaminate.
How can I make or meat or drink my care,
How can mine eyes enjoy
The light of day, when I see ravens tear
Thy eagles' flesh, and dogs thy lions' whelps destroy?
Away! thou cup of sorrow's poisoned gall!
Scarce can my soul thy bitterness sustain.
When I Ahola unto mind recall,

I taste thy venom; and when once again
Upon Aholiba I muse, thy dregs I drain.

Perfect in beauty, Zion! how in thee
Do love and grace unite!
The souls of thy companions tenderly
Turn unto thee; thy joy was their delight,
And, weeping, they lament thy ruin now.
In distant exile, for thy sacred height
They long, and toward thy gates in prayer they bow.
Thy flocks are scattered o'er the barren waste,
Yet do they not forget thy sheltering fold,
Unto thy garments' fringe they cling, and haste
The branches of thy palms to seize and hold.
Shinar and Pathros! come they near to thee?
Naught are they by thy Light and Right divine.
To what can be compared the majesty
Of thy anointed line?
To what the singers, seers, and Levites thine?
The rule of idols fails and is cast down,
Thy power eternal is, from age to age thy crown.

The Lord desires thee for his dwelling-place
Eternally; and blest
Is he whom God has chosen for the grace
Within thy courts to rest.
Happy is he that watches, drawing near,
Until he sees thy glorious lights arise,
And over whom thy dawn breaks full and clear
Set in the Orient skies.
But happiest he, who, with exultant eyes,
The bliss of thy redeemed ones shall behold,
And see thy youth renewed as in the days of old.

GOD, WHOM SHALL I COMPARE TO THEE?

God! whom shall I compare to thee,
When thou to none canst likened be?

Under what image shall I dare
To picture thee, when ev'rywhere
All Nature's forms thine impress bear?

Greater, O Lord! thy glories are
Than all the heavenly chariot far.
Whose mind can grasp thy world's design?
Whose word can fitly thee define?
Whose tongue set forth thy powers divine?

Can heart approach, can eye behold
Thee in thy righteousness untold?
Whom didst thou to thy counsel call,
When there was none to speak withal
Since thou wast first and Lord of all?

Thy world eternal witness bears
That none its Maker's glory shares.
Thy wisdom is made manifest
In all things formed by thy behest,
All with thy seal's clear mark imprest.

Before the pillars of the sky
Were raised, before the mountains high
Were wrought, ere hills and dales were known,
Thou in thy majesty alone
Didst sit, O God! upon thy throne!

Hearts, seeking thee, from search refrain,
And weary tongues their praise restrain.
Thyself unbound by time and place,
Thou dost pervade, support, embrace
The world and all created space.

The sages' minds bewildered grow,
The lightning-speed of thought is slow.
" Awful in praises " art thou named;
Thou fillest, strong in strength proclaimed,
This universe thy hand has framed.

Deep, deep beyond all fathoming,
Far, far beyond all measuring,
We can but seek thy deeds alone;
When bow thy saints before thy throne
Then is thy faithfulness made known.

Thy righteousness we can discern,
Thy holy law proclaim and learn.
Is not thy presence near alway
To them who penitently pray,
But far from those who sinning stray?

Pure souls behold thee, and no need
Have they of light: they hear and heed
Thee with the mind's keen ear, although
The ear of flesh be dull and slow.
Their voices answer to and fro.

Thy holiness forever they proclaim:
The Lord of Hosts! thrice holy is his name!

SERVANT OF GOD

Oh! would that I might be
A servant unto thee,
Thou God by all adored:
Then, though by friends out-cast,
Thy hand would hold me fast,
And draw me near to thee, my King and Lord!

Spirit and flesh are thine,
O Heavenly Shepherd mine!
My hopes, my thoughts, my fears, thou seest all,
Thou measurest my path, my steps dost know.
When thou upholdest, who can make me fall?
When thou restrainest, who can bid me go?
Oh! would that I might be
A servant unto thee,

Thou God, by all adored.
Then, though by friends out-cast,
Thy hand would hold me fast,
And draw me near to thee, my King and Lord!

Fain would my heart come nigh
To thee, O God! on high,
But evil thoughts have led me far astray
From the pure path of righteous government.
Guide thou me back into thy holy way,
And count me not as one impenitent.
Oh! would that I might be
A servant unto thee,
Thou God, by all adored.
Then, though by friends out-cast,
Thy hand would hold me fast,
And draw me near to thee, my King and Lord!

If in my youth I still
Fail to perform thy will,
What can I hope when age shall chill my breast?
Heal me, O Lord! with thee is healing found —
Cast me not off, by weight of years opprest,
Forsake me not when age my strength has bound.
Oh! would that I might be
A servant unto thee,
Thou God, by all adored.
Then, though by friends out-cast,
Thy hand would hold me fast,
And draw me near to thee, my King and Lord!

Contrite and full of dread,
I mourn each moment fled
Midst idle follies roaming desolate;
I sink beneath transgressions manifold,
That from thy presence keep me separate;
Nor can sin-darkened eyes thy light behold.
Oh! would that I might be

A servant unto thee,
Thou God, by all adored.
Then, though by friends out-cast,
Thy hand would hold me fast,
And draw me near to thee, my King and Lord!

So lead me that I may
Thy sovereign will obey.
Make pure my heart to seek thy truth divine;
When burns my wound, be thou with healing near!
Answer me, Lord! for sore distress is mine,
And say unto thy servant, I am here!
Oh! would that I might be
A servant unto thee,
Thou God, by all adored!
Then, though by friends out-cast,
Thy hand would hold me fast,
And draw me near to thee, my King and Lord!

TO THE SOUL

O thou, who springest gloriously
   From thy Creator's fountain blest,
   Arise, depart, for this is not thy rest!
The way is long, thou must preparèd be,
   Thy Maker bids thee seek thy goal —
   Return then to thy rest, my soul,
For bountifully has God dealt with thee.

Behold! I am a stranger here,
   My days like fleeting shadows seem.
   When wilt thou, if not now, thy life redeem?
And when thou seek'st thy Maker have no fear,
   For if thou have but purified
   Thy heart from stain of sin and pride,
Thy righteous deeds to him shall draw thee near.

O thou in strength who treadest, learn
   To know thyself, cast dreams away!

The goal is distant far, and short the day.
What canst thou plead th' Almighty's grace to earn?
  Would thou the glory of the Lord
  Behold, O soul?   With prompt accord
Then to thy Father's house return, return!

O SLEEPER! WAKE, ARISE!

O sleeper! wake, arise!
  Delusive follies shun,
Keep from the ways of men and raise thine eyes
  To the exalted One.
Hasten as haste the starry orbs of gold
  To serve the Rock of old.
O sleeper! rise and call upon thy God!

Behold the firmament
  His hands have wrought on high,
See how his mighty arms uphold the tent
  Of his ethereal sky,
And mark the host of stars that heaven reveals —
His graven rings and seals.
Tremble before his majesty and hope
  For his salvation still,
Lest, when for thee the gates of fortune ope,
  False pride thy spirit fill.
O sleeper! rise and call upon thy God!

Go seek at night abroad
  Their footsteps, who erewhile
Were saints on earth, whose lips with hymns o'erflowed,
  Whose hearts were free from guilt.
Their nights were spent in ceaseless prayer and praise,
  In pious fast their days.
Their souls were paths to God, and by his throne
  Their place is set anigh.
Their road through life was but a stepping-stone
  Unto the Lord on high.
O sleeper! rise and call upon thy God!

Weep for thy sins, and pause
   In wrongful deeds, to implore
God's pardoning grace, nor fret thyself because
   Of evil-doers more.
Cleave to the right, and of thy substance bring
   To honor him, thy King.
When saviors then Mount Zion joyfully
   Ascend with eager feet,
And nations shout for gladness, thou wilt be
   Prepared thy God to meet.
O sleeper! rise and call upon thy God!

Whence does man's wisdom flow —
   Man, who of dust is wrought,
Whose poor pre-eminence on earth does show
   Over the beast as naught?
Only those gazing with the inward eye
   Behold God's majesty:
They have the well-spring of their being found,
   More precious far than wine.
Thou also thus, though by earth's fetters bound,
   Mayst find thy Rock divine.
O sleeper! rise and call upon thy God!

The Lord is Lord of all,
   His hands hold life and death,
He bids the lowly rise, the lofty fall,
   The world obeys his breath.
Keep judgment, then, and live and cast aside
   False and rebellious pride,
That asketh when and where, and all below
   And all above would know;
But be thou perfect with the Lord thy God!
O sleeper! rise and call upon thy God!

THE HEART'S DESIRE

Lord! unto thee are ever manifest
My inmost heart's desires, though unexprest

In spoken words.   Thy mercy I implore
Even for a moment — then to die were blest.

Oh! if I might but win that grace divine,
Into thy hand, O Lord, I would resign
My spirit then, and lay me down in peace
To my repose, and sweetest sleep were mine.

Afar from thee in midst of life I die,
And life in death I find, when thou art nigh.
Alas! I know not how to seek thy face,
Nor how to serve and worship thee, Most High.

Oh! lead me in thy path, and turn again
My heart's captivity, and break in twain
The yoke of folly: teach me to afflict
My soul, the while I yet life's strength retain.

Despise not thou my lowly penitence,
Ere comes the day, when, deadened every sense,
My limbs too feeble grown to bear my weight,
A burden to myself, I journey hence.

When to the all-consuming moth a prey,
My wasted form sinks slowly to decay,
And I shall seek the place my fathers sought,
And find my rest there where at rest are they.

I am on earth a sojourner, a guest,
And my inheritance is in her breast,
My youth has sought as yet its own desires,
When will my soul's true welfare be my quest?

The world is too much with me, and its din
Prevents my search eternal peace to win.
How can I serve my Maker when my heart
Is passion's captive, is a slave to sin?

But should I strive to scale ambition's height,
Who with the worm may sleep ere fall of night?
Or can I joy in happiness to-day
Who know not what may chance by morning's light?

My days and nights will soon, with restless speed,
Consume life's remnant yet to me decreed;
Then half my body shall the winds disperse,
Half will return to dust, as dust indeed.

What more can I allege?   From youth to age
Passion pursues me still at every stage.
If thou art not my portion, what is mine?
Lacking thy favor, what my heritage?

Bare of good deeds, scorched by temptation's fire,
Yet to thy mercy dares my soul aspire;
But wherefore speech prolong, since unto Thee,
O Lord, is manifest my heart's desire?

HYMN FOR PENTECOST

When thou didst descend upon Sinai's mountain,
It trembled and shook 'neath thy mighty hand,
And the rocks were moved by thy power and splendor;
How then can my spirit before thee stand
On the day when darkness o'erspread the heavens,
And the sun was hidden at thy command?
The angels of God, for thy great name's worship,
Are ranged before thee, a shining band,
And the children of men are waiting ever
Thy mercies unnumbered as grains of sand;
The law they received from the mouth of thy glory,
They learn and consider and understand.
Oh! accept thou their song and rejoice in their gladness,
Who proclaim thy glory in every land.

GOD AND MAN

O Lord! I will declare
Thy holy name, thy glories past compare:
My tongue shall not conceal, O Lord!
Thy righteousness made known to me:
I heard and I believed thy word,
I will not ask presumptuously.
For should the vase of clay
" What doest thou ? " unto its maker say ?
Him have I sought and known,
A rock of strength, a tower of might,
Resplendent as the glorious light,
Without or veil or covering, radiant shown:
Exalted, magnified,
        Extolled and glorified.

The heavens from hour to hour
Declare thy wondrous works, proclaim thy power;
Sunrise and sunset, still the same,
Prostrate in awe eternally.
The angels pass through flood and flame
As unto thee they testify;
Thy praise they celebrate,
O thou, the fruit of lips who dost create.
For thou uphold'st alone,
Unwearied and invisible,
The depths, the heights, where move and dwell
The living creatures and the heavenly throne:
Exalted, magnified,
        Extolled and glorified.

Who has the glory praised
Fitly of him, whose word the heavens upraised ?
The Eternal One, who dwells concealed
In his exalted heights, but yet
In Zion's temple, full revealed,
Did erst his glorious presence set,
And he showed visions then

To cause his image to be seen of men;
Yet past all measuring
His wisdom is, past depth and height
He flashes on his prophet's sight
In visions only as the heavenly king:
Exalted, magnified,
          Extolled and glorified.

His power, exceeding great,
Is without end: who can his praise narrate?
Happy the man, who testifies
Unto his greatness manifold,
Whose faith in God unshaken lies,
In God, whose arms the world uphold,
Who, fearing God, can trust
In Him, acknowledging his deeds are just,
That for himself has he
Made all his works, his creatures all,
And that his awful day will call
All men, the judgment of their deeds to see:
Exalted, magnified,
          Extolled and glorified.

Do thou then heed and learn,
Prepare thyself thy nature to discern.
See whence thou comest, what thou art,
And who created thee and taught
Thee knowledge, and in every part
Of thee the power of motion wrought.
Mark then God's might untold,
And rouse thyself his wonders to behold.
But to himself concealed
Dare not to stretch thy hand, for then
Thou seekest, with presumptuous ken,
The first and last, the hidden and revealed:
Exalted, magnified,
          Extolled and glorified.

PASSOVER HYMN

When as a wall the sea
  In heaps uplifted lay,
A new song unto thee
  Sang the redeemed that day.

Thou didst in his deceit
  O'erwhelm the Egyptian's feet,
While Israel's footsteps fleet
  How beautiful were they!

Jeshurun! all who see
  Thy glory cry to thee:
"Who like thy God can be?"
  Thus even our foes did say.

Oh! let thy banner soar
  The scattered remnant o'er,
And gather them once more
  Like corn on harvest day.

Who bear through all their line
  Thy covenant's holy sign,
And to thy name divine
  Are sanctified alway.

Let all the world behold
  Their token, prized of old,
Who on their garments' fold
  The thread of blue display.

Be then the truth made known
  For whom, and whom alone,
The twisted fringe is shown,
  The covenant kept this day.

Oh! let them, sanctified,
  Once more with thee abide,

Their sun shine far and wide,
 And chase the clouds away.

The well-beloved declare
 Thy praise and song and prayer:
" Who can with thee compare,
 O Lord of Hosts?" they say.

When as a wall the sea
 In heaps unlifted lay,
A new song unto thee
 Sang the redeemed that day.

MORNING PRAYER

O Lord! my life was known to thee
Ere thou hadst caused me yet to be,
Thy Spirit ever dwells in me.

Could I, cast down by thee, have gained
A standing place, or, if restrained
By thee, go forth with feet unchained?

Hear me, Almighty, while I pray,
My thoughts are in thy hand alway,
Be to my helplessness a stay!

Oh! may this hour thy favor yield,
And may I tread life's battle-field
Encompassed by thy mercy's shield.

Wake me at dawn thy name to bless,
And in thy sanctuary's recess
To praise and laud thy holiness.

This is the end of this publication.

Any remaining blank pages are for our book binding requirements and are blank on purpose.

To search thousands of interesting publications like this one, please remember to visit our website at:

http://www.kessinger.net

CPSIA information can be obtained at www.ICGtesting.com
Printed in the USA
BVOW09s1953170215

388157BV00017B/386/P